Etta Jenks

Marlane Meyer

The Royal Court Writers Series published by Methuen Drama in association with the Royal Court Theatre

Royal Court Writers Series

Etta Jenks *was first published in Great Britain in the Royal Court Writers Series in 1990 by Methuen Drama, Michelin House, 81 Fulham Road, London SW3 6RB in association with the Royal Court Theatre, Sloane Square, London SW1N 8AS and distributed in the United States of America by HEB Inc., 361 Hanover Street, Portsmouth, New Hampshire 03801.*

A CIP catalogue record for this book is available from the British Library.

ISBN 0-413-65160-6

Printed in England by Clays Ltd, St Ives plc

The illustration on the front cover is from the Royal Court Theatre poster by Strong.

This script went to press a month before the première of **Etta Jenks.**

THE ENGLISH STAGE COMPANY
AT THE
ROYAL COURT

The history of the English Stage Company is generally held to have begun with the seminal production of John Osborne's *LOOK BACK IN ANGER* in May 1956. Since then, the Royal Court has consistently been the flagship of new writing and the principal home of the theatrical avant garde in this country.

First and foremost a theatre of new writing, the aim of the English Stage Company is to develop and produce the best in new writing for the theatre, encouraging writers from all sections of society to address the problems of our times. Early Court writers included: John Osborne, Arnold Wesker, John Arden, David Storey, Ann Jellicoe and Edward Bond. They were followed by a generation of writers led by David Hare and Howard Brenton and, in more recent years, the celebrated house writers have included Caryl Churchill, Timberlake Wertenbaker and Robert Holman.

In line with the policy of nurturing new writing, the Theatre Upstairs has mainly been seen as a place for exploration and experiment, where writers can hone their craft prior to the demands of the Mainstage auditorium. This has proved successful over the years and recent graduates to have moved from Upstairs to Down include Andrea Dunbar, Sarah Daniels, Jim Cartwright, Clare McIntyre and Timberlake Wertenbaker. In recent years, rehearsed readings and workshops have sometimes been used to start the collaboration between writer, director and actors at an earlier point. Plays like *SERIOUS MONEY* or *OUR COUNTRY'S GOOD* were both written following periods of workshop research.

But, despite recent box office successes such as *SERIOUS MONEY, ROAD, OUR COUNTRY'S GOOD, MY MOTHER SAID I NEVER SHOULD, MY HEART'S A SUITCASE* and *A WHISTLE IN THE DARK;* the 80's have been a period of diminished productivity as funding levels generally have declined. In particular, the English Stage Company has been unable to gain any substantial support from our local authority, the Royal Borough of Kensington and Chelsea. Last year the Theatre Upstairs was closed for 8 months. However, the English Stage Company has received a generous uplift from the Arts Council for the current year and, in May, the Theatre Upstairs re-opened for a season of work under the festival title of "May Days". This season presented 15 short, specially commissioned plays on topics of immediate social and political importance. But, despite this positive step, as the English Stage Company moves into the 1990's, it is alarmingly clear that the business of promoting new writing in the theatre is as precarious as ever. It is this knowledge coupled with commitment that gives the Royal Court a certain edge. And, as always, it is a mixture of idealism and pragmatism that will ensure the survival of the English Stage Company.

PRODUCTION

Directed by	**Max Stafford-Clark**
Designed by	**William Dudley**
Lighting by	**Mark Henderson**
Sound by	**Bryan Bowen**
Voice Coach	**Joan Washington**
Costume Supervisor	**Jennifer Cook**
Assistant Director	**Catriona Taylor**
Stage Manager	**Gemma Bodley**
Deputy Stage Manager	**Gary Crant**
Assistant Stage Manager	**Jill Biffin**
Production Photography	**John Haynes**
Leaflet designed by	**Sightlines**
Poster designed by	**Strong**

ETTA JENKS was originally produced by Los Angeles Theatre Center, Bill Bushnell, Artistic Producing Director and the Women's Project and Productions, Inc. Julia Miles, Artistic Director.

Wardrobe care by PERSIL and COMFORT, Adhesive by COPYDEX and EVODE LTD, Ioniser for the lighting control room by THE LONDON IONISER CENTRE (836 0211), Cordless drill by MAKITA ELECTRIC (UK) LTD, Watches by THE TIMEX CORPORATION, Batteries by EVER READY, Refrigerators by ELECTROLUX and PHILIPS MAJOR APPLIANCES LTD, Microwave by TOSHIBA UK LTD, Kettles for rehearsals by MORPHY RICHARDS, Video for casting purposes by HITACHI, Cold bottled beer at the bar supplied by YOUNG & CO BREWERY, WANDSWORTH, Coffee machine by CONA. Furniture by KNOLL INTERNATIONAL.

Microwave for backstage use kindly supplied by ELECTROLUX , Freezer for backstage use supplied by ZANUSSI LTD "Now that's a good idea"; Camera and monitor by MITSUBISHI UK LTD; thanks to CASIO for the use of DAT equipment.

Persons shall not be permitted to stand or sit in any of the gangways intersecting the seating or to sit in any of the other gangways. The Management reserves the right to refuse admission and to make any alteration in the cast which may be rendered necessary by any illness or other unavoidable causes. Patrons are reminded that smoking is not permitted in the auditorium. No photographs to be taken or tape recordings to be made.

FUNDED BY
THE ROYAL BOROUGH OF
KENSINGTON AND CHELSEA

THE ROYAL COURT THEATRE

presents

ETTA JENKS

by

Marlane Meyer

In order of appearance:

ETTA	Miranda Richardson
BURT	Lennie James
CLYDE	Pearce Quigley
BEN	David Rintoul
DOLLY	Debora Weston
SHERI	Debora Weston
SHERMAN	Lennie James
SPENCER	Robin Soans
KITTY	Sara Stewart
DWIGHT	Pearce Quigley
JAMES	Christopher Fairbank
ALEC	Lennie James
MAX	Christopher Fairbank
SHELLY	Sara Stewart

BIOGRAPHIES

BRYAN BOWEN – Resident Sound Designer at the Royal Court where work includes: *Our Country's Good, Ice Cream, Beside Herself, My Heart's A Suitcase, My Mother Said I Never Should, Gibraltar Strait, Falkland Sound, Blood.* Other theatre includes: *Ghosts, A Touch of the Poet, Outbreak of God In Area Nine, A Midsummer Night's Dream, Julius Caesar, Romeo and Juliet* (Young Vic); *Mummy, Trafford Tanzi* (Bubble Theatre).

WILLIAM DUDLEY – For the Royal Court: *Small Change, The Fool, Hamlet, Edmond, Kafka's Dick.* Other theatre includes: *Lavender Blue, Larkrise to Candleford, Lost Worlds, The World Turned Upsidedown, Spirit of '76, Undiscovered Country, Dispatches, Don Quixote, Schweyk in the Second World War, The Mysteries, The Real Inspector Hound, The Critic, Entertaining Strangers, Waiting For Godot, Cat on a Hot Tin Roof, The Shaughraun, The Voysey Inheritance, The Changeling, Bartholemew Fair, The Crucible* , (National Theatre); *Marya* (Old Vic); *Ivanov, That Good Between Us, Richard III, The Party, The Merry Wives of Windsor, Richard II, A Midsummer Night's Dream (RSC); The Ship* (Glasgow's Cultural City 1990). Opera work includes: *Anna Christie, The Barber of Seville (WNO) Tales of Hoffman, Der Rosenkavilier, Don Giovanni, The Cunning Little Vixen* (ROH); *A Masked Ball* (Salzburg).

CHRISTOPHER FAIRBANK – For the Royal Court: *The Lucky Chance, Irish Eyes and English Tears.* Other theatre includes: *A Study in Scarlet* (Greenwich); *Blues For Mr Charlie* (Crucible, Sheffield); *The Misanthrope* (Cambridge Theatre Company); *Nightshade* (King's Head); *Psychosis Unclassified* (New York/Bush Theatre); *Flying Blind* (Everyman, Liverpool); *The Wedding Feast* (Birmingham Rep); *Romeo and Juliet* (Newcastle Playhouse); *Illuminatus* (Cottesloe). TV includes: *South of the Border, Rockliffe's Babies, Casualty, Bergerac, The Old Curiosity Shop* (BBC); *The Bill* (Thames); *Auf Wiedersehen Pet* (Central). Film includes: *Hamlet* (Marquis Films); *White Hunter Black Heart, Batman, Agatha* (Warner); *Venus Peter* (British Film Institute).

MARK HENDERSON – For the Royal Court; *My Mother Said I Never Should, Edmond, Kafka's Dick.* Other theatre includes: *Mephisto, A Midsummer Night's Dream, The Churchill Play, Richard II, Macbeth, Penny For A Song, Kiss Me Kate, Measure For Measure, Much Ado About Nothing, The Tempest* (RSC); *Cat On A Hot Tin Roof, The Shaughraun, The Changeling, The Magical Olympical Games, Hedda Gabler, Hamlet, The Beaux Stratagem, Ma Rainey's Black Bottom, The Voysey Inheritance, Whale, Racing Demon* (National Theatre); Numerous London West End credits include: *Mutiny, Arturo Ui, Follies, Beyond Reasonable Doubt, The Sneeze, Gasping.* Opera credits include productions for ENO, National Opera Studio, Scottish Opera, Opera North, Hong Kong Festival and Opera de Nancy. Ballet credits include: Ballet Rambert, London Contemporary Dance, Sadlers Wells, Royal Ballet.

LENNIE JAMES – Theatre includes: *Ma Rainey's Black Bottom* (National Theatre); *The Merchant of Venice* (Wolsey, Ipswich); *Black Ice* (Derby Playhouse); *No Two Ways, Something's Burning* (Lyric, Hammersmith); *Waking Hours* (Lyric, Library Theatre Manchester); *Short Eyes* (Man in the Moon); *Hamlet* (Shaw Theatre); *Colossus, Just Good Friends* (Cockpit). TV includes: *The Orchid House* (Channel 4); *Between The Cracks, Something's Burning, Chilling Out* (BBC).

PEARCE QUIGLEY – For the Royal Court: *Downfall.* Other theatre includes: *Lady From The Sea, Twelfth Night, Salonika,* (Duke's Lancaster); *A Winter's Tale, The Park* (Crucible, Sheffield); *Abingdon Square* (Soho Poly/Cottesloe); *Hot Fudge and Ice Cream* (Manchester Contact) *Inspector Morse* (Zenith) *A Perfect Hero* (LWT). Film includes: *Killing Dad, Ladder of Swords.*

MIRANDA RICHARDSON – For the Royal Court: *A Lie of the Mind, Edmond*. Other theatre includes: *Mountain Language, The Changeling* (National); *Moving* (Queen's Theatre); *Insignificance, The Maids, Who's Afraid of Virginia Woolf, The Table of Two Horsemen* (Bristol Old Vic); *Educating Rita* (Leicester Haymarket); *Stags and Hens* (Duke's, Lancaster); *Savage Amusement, All My Sons, Sisterly Feelings* (Derby Playhouse); *Whose Life Is It Anyway?, Play It Again Sam, Ten Times Table, Return of AJ Raffles, Tom Jones* (Manchester Library). TV includes: *The Master Builder, Black Adder II, Black Adder III, After Pilkington, Lucky Jim, Die Kinder* (BBC); *Death of the Heart, Demon Lover* (Granada); *The Storyteller/Jim Henson, Secret Friends/10x10,* (Channel 4) Film includes: *Dance With A Stranger* (First Films); *Empire of the Sun* (Warner Bros); *The Innocent* (BBC Films); *The Mad Monkey* (Iberoamericana Films), *Dr Grasler, The Fool*.

DAVID RINTOUL – For the Royal Court: *Sergeant Ola and His Followers*. Other theatre includes: *Fanshen, Speakers, Yesterday's News, Devil's Island, It's a Mad World My Masters, Epsom Downs, An Optimistic Thrust* (Joint Stock); *The World Turned Upside Down, The Trojan War Will Not Take Place, A Midsummer Night's Dream, The Rivals* (National Theatre); *Henry IV Parts I & II* (RSC Tour) *Candida, Macbeth* (Old Vic Tour);' *The Beaux Stratagem, Infidelities* (Lyric, Hammersmith); *Absolute Hell* (Orange Tree); *Richard II, Richard III* (Phoenix Theatre). TV includes: *The Cherry Orchard, Shadow of the Noose, Pride and Prejudice, The Dunroamin' Rising* (BBC), *The Mysterious Affair at Styles* (LWT), *Taggart* (STV). Film includes: *The Legend of the Werewolf*.

ROBIN SOANS – For the Royal Court: *Bed of Roses*. Other theatre includes: *Fashion* (Leicester Haymarket/Tricycle); *Germinal, Berlin Days Hollywood Nights* (Place Theatre /Tour); *Bet Noir* (Young Vic); *Thatcher's Women* (Tricycle Theatre/Tour); *Gringo Planet* (Gate Theatre) *Pricksong for the New Leviathan* (Old Red Lion), *Journey's End, Romeo and Juliet, Bomb in Brewery Street, Charley's Aunt* (Crucible Theatre); TV includes: *The Last Place on Earth, Tales of Sherwood Forest* (Central); *This Land of England* (Channel 4); *Racing Game* (Yorkshire); *Chelworth, Lord Peter Wimsey, Bergerac* (BBC); Film includes: *Absolution, Hidden City, The Patricia Neal Story, Comrades*.

MAX STAFFORD-CLARK is Artistic Director of the English Stage Company at the Royal Court Theatre.

SARA STEWART – Trained at Central. Theatre includes: *The Doll's House* (Rose Tavern, London); *Fertility Dance* (Nuffield, Southampton); *Lady Windemere's Fan, While The Sun Shines, Dear Brutus, Sly Fox, Witness for the Prosecution* (Pitlochry Festival Theatre); *The Real World?* (Soho Poly); *Temptation* (Westminster). TV includes: *Drop the Dead Donkey* (Hat Trick Productions).

DEBORA WESTON – Theatre includes: *Serious Money* (Wyndhams Theatre); *Scheherazade* (Soho Poly); *Uncle Vanya* (Theatre Royal, Plymouth); *Golden Leaf Strut* (White Bear Theatre); *The Misanthrope* (Judith Andersen Theatre, New York); *Open Admissions* (Lehman Theatre, New York); *Three Sisters* (Hartford Theatre, Connecticut). TV includes: *Magic Moments* (Yorkshire); *Coded Hostile* (Granada); *The Big Knife* (HTV); *Final Warning* (TNT). Film includes: *Nightbreed, Shining Through, A Birthday Fish*.

THE OLIVIER APPEAL

Laurence Olivier 1907 - 1989
(Snowdon)

The Royal Court Theatre was very proud of Lord Olivier's patronage of our Appeal. It will continue in his name as a memorial to his life and talent.
The Appeal was launched in June 1988 - the Royal Court's 100th anniversary year. The target is £800,000 to repair and refurbish the theatre and to enable the English Stage Company to maintain and continue its worldwide reputation as Britain's "National Theatre of new writing".

The Royal Court would like to thank the following for their generous contributions to the Appeal:

Abbey Life
Edgar Astaire
The Hon. M.L. Astor's 1969 Charitable Trust
Associated British Foods
Sir Richard Attenborough
The Clifford Barclay Trust
Olivier Berggruen
Phyllis Blackburn
The Elaine and Neville Blond Charitable Trust
Paul Brooke
Christopher Campbell
Carole Catto
The John S. Cohen Foundation
The Cowdray Trust
D'Oyley Carte Charitable Trust
David Croser
The Douglas Heath Eves Trust
The Economist
Mr and Mrs Nicholas Egon
The Esmee Fairbairn Trust
Essekte Letraser
Matthew Evans
Evans and Reiss
Robert Flemming & Company

D J Freeman & Company
Brian Friel
Michael Frayn
Gala (100th Anniversary)
Collette Gleeson
The Godinton Trust
Lord Goodman
Christopher Hampton
Hatter (IMO) Foundation
The Hedley Trust
Anthony and Jennifer Hopkins
Claude Hug
Mrs P.P. Hyde
The Inchape Charitable Trust Fund
Jacob's Island Co plc
The John Lewis Partnership
Bernard Krichefski
Perry Kershaw Ltd
The Kobler Trust
Eddie Kulukundis
The London and Edinburgh Trust
The Mercers
Midgley Snelling & Co.
Portia Mores
Anna Louise Neuberg Trust
Richard Nickols
National Westminster Bank plc

Olivier Banquet
Peter Jones
The Pilgrim Trust
Pirelli Ltd
Irene Pruller-Daff
A.J.R.Purssell
Mr and Mrs J.A.Pye's Charitable Settlement
St Quentin Ltd
The Rayne Foundation
Lady Richardson
Mrs Ruth Rogers
The Lord Sainsbury Trust
Save & Prosper Group plc
Andrew Sinclair
Wing Commander and Mrs Sinclair
1964 Charitable Trust
W.H.Smith & Son
The Spencer-Wills Trust
Max Stafford-Clark
"Stormy Monday" Charity Premiere
Tracey Ullman
Andrew Wadsworth
Timothy West and Prunella Scales
Anthony Wilson
Irene Worth

THE ROYAL COURT THEATRE SOCIETY

For many years now Members of the Royal Court Theatre Society have received special notice of new productions, but why not become a Friend, Associate or a Patron of the Royal Court, thereby involving yourself directly in maintaining the high standard and unique quality of Royal Court productions - while enjoying complimentary tickets to the shows themselves?

Subscriptions run for one year; to become a Member costs £12, a Friend £60 (joint) £40 (single), an Associate £400, a Patron £1,000.

PATRONS Diana Bliss, Caryl Churchill, Issac Davidov, Alfred Davis, Forsyte Kerman, Lady Eileen Joseph, Stonewall Productions Ltd., Tracey Ullman, Timberlake Wertenbaker, Irene Worth.

ASSOCIATES J. Astor, David Capelli, Michael Codron, Jeremy Conway, Mrs Henny Gestetner, London Arts Discovery Tours, Patricia Marmont, Barbara Minto, David Mirvish, Nick Hern Books, Greville Poke, Jane Rayne, Sir Dermot de Trafford, Megan Willis.

CORPORATE PATRONS Amersham International, B.A.A Plc.

Marlane Meyer

COMING NEXT

MAIN HOUSE

From 4th January
ALL THINGS NICE
by Sharman Macdonald
Directed by Max Stafford-Clark
Sharman Macdonald's past plays include **THE BRAVE** and the award winning
WHEN I WAS A GIRL I USED TO SCREAM AND SHOUT

THEATRE UPSTAIRS

5 - 10 November
Gay Sweatshop production of
KITCHEN MATTERS
by Bryony Lavery
Directed by Nona Shepphard

22 November - 15 December
NO ONE SEES THE VIDEO
by Martin Crimp
Directed by Lindsay Posner

7 - 12 January
The Royal Court Theatre and
Royal National Theatre present
THE FEVER
by Wallace Shawn
A monologue directed and performed by **Wallace Shawn**
PRIOR TO A NATIONAL TOUR

FOR THE ROYAL COURT

DIRECTION

Artistic Director	**Max Stafford-Clark**
Associate Director	**Lindsay Posner**
Casting Director	**Lisa Makin**
Literary Manager	**Melanie Kenyon**
Artistic Assistant	**Helen Carter**
Resident Playwright	**Victoria Hardie**
Gerald Chapman Award Trainee Director	**Catriona Taylor**

PRODUCTION

Production Manager	**Bo Barton**
Chief Electrician	**Johanna Town**
Deputy Chief Electrician	**Matthew O'Connor**
Electrician	**Denis O'Hare***
Master Carpenter	**Guy Viggers**
Deputy Master Carpenter	**John Stritch**
Technical Manager, Theatre Upstairs	**Chris Samuels**
Sound Designer	**Bryan Bowen**
Board Operators	**Jonquil Pantin***
	Steve Hepworth*
Wardrobe Supervisor	**Jennifer Cook**
Deputy Wardrobe Supervisor	**Iona Kenrick**

ADMINISTRATION

General Manager	**Graham Cowley**
Assistant to General Manager	**Georgia Cheales**
Finance Administrator	**Mark Rubinstein**
Finance Assistant	**Rachel Harrison**
Press (071 730 2652)	**Judith Dimant**
Marketing and Publicity Manager	**Guy Chapman**
Sales Manager	**Nicki Shindler**
Development Manager	**Anne-Marie Thompson**
Development Assistant	**Nina Dawson**
House Manager	**Gambol Parker**
Deputy House Manager	**Alison Smith**
Box Office Manager	**Joe Brooking**
Box Office Assistants	**Rachel Foster**
	Rita Sharma
Stage Door/Telephonists	**Peter Kaestner***
	Jan Noyce*
Evening Stage Door	**Tyrone Lucas***
Maintenance	**John Lorrigio***
Cleaners	**Eileen Chapman***
	Ivy Jones*
Firemen	**Martin Dicks***
	Paul Kleinmann*
	Clive Lewis*

YOUNG PEOPLE'S THEATRE

Director	**Elyse Dodgson**
Administrator	**Dominic Tickell**

* Part-time staff

The ape, alone in his bamboo cage, smells

The python, and cries, but no one hears him call.
The grave moves forward from its ambush,
Curling slowly, with sideways motion,
Passing under bushes and through leaf tunnels,

Leaving dogs and sheep murdered where it slept.
Some shining thing inside us, that has
Served us well, shakes its bamboo bars.
It may be gone before we wake.

                    --From "Defeated" by Robert Bly

MATERIALS FOR THE PLAY

Playwright's Note

With the exception of Etta, Burt and Sherman, the characters
should all be possessed of a certain animal quality, subtly
suggested through makeup or gesture. The effect should not be
cartoonish, but queer. The landscape should suggest the kind
of contained isolation that might be found in an empty
acquarium at an abandoned sea park.

CHARACTERS

ETTA JENKS, a woman in her early 30s.

CLYDE, a man in his mid-30s.

BURT, a man in his late 20s, deaf.

SHERMAN, Burt's twin brother, blind.

BEN, a man in his 40s.

DOLLY, a woman in her 40s.

DWIGHT, a man in his late 20s.

JAMES, a man in his late 20s.

SPENCER, a man in his early 50s.

SHERI, a woman in her mid-30s.

KITTY, a woman in her early 20s.

ALEC, a man in his early 20s.

MAX, a man in his late 30s.

SHELLY, a young girl, 18.

The play can be performed by four women and five men with doubling.

Scene 1

Darkness. A train whistle blows in the distance.
The engine becomes audible.
A covered light hangs down at center stage. It comes
up to reveal ETTA standing on a small platform. SHE
wears a long coat and carries a large suitcase. SHE
seems to be leaning into the sound of the train,
waiting, as the train approaches. The lights flicker,
and start flashing as the sound of the train roars by.
ETTA disappears in a blackout. The train sound recedes
in the distance.
The lights come up on a bare stage. We hear the
sounds of a busy train terminal: a voice announcing
arrivals and departures, people milling, voices calling
to each other. ETTA is center stage. SHE pulls a map
from her purse. A young man enters with a load of
luggage, a baggage handler (BURT). HE glances at her
briefly before unloading the luggage. A man approaches;
his name is CLYDE.

CLYDE (To ETTA): How you doin'... (SHE moves away) Excuse
me. (SHE moves away) Miss? Excuse me...but....Miss? I
can see you're from out of town...

ETTA: Please don't. (SHE moves away)

CLYDE: I see you have what looks like a map?

ETTA: No.

CLYDE: Well it sure looks like a map.

ETTA (Approaches BURT): Could you help me?

CLYDE: I could help you.

ETTA: Please leave me alone.

BURT: I have to see your lips when you talk.

    CLYDE steps between BURT and ETTA.

CLYDE: I'm insanely good with a map, like the army was havin'
a hard time trainin' their guys to read a map? And they
heard how good I was and they snapped me out of civilian
life, bad knee, I had a metal plate in my head, they did not
care 'cause I'm so good with a map, they flang me smack to
the middle of Nam...

ETTA (To BURT): I fell asleep and I don't know where I am.

CLYDE: Angel City.

BURT: Los Angeles.

ETTA (To BURT): I am looking for someplace to stay, someplace cheap.

CLYDE: I know just the place, let me help you with your bag.

>   ETTA and CLYDE struggle with the bag.

BURT: Like a motel.

ETTA: I'd like it to be cheap.

CLYDE: You can stay with me for nothin'...

BURT: You got any money?

ETTA: Not a lot.

CLYDE: I got a lot of money and I can show <u>you</u> how to get a lot of money...

BURT: Say again...?

CLYDE: Meeting successful businessmen...

ETTA: I have some money.

CLYDE: Eating at expensive restaurants...

BURT: I have a brother might be able to rent you a place. You'd have to be out during the day.

ETTA: Out where?

CLYDE: Out on your ass.

BURT: Wherever it is people go when they're not home.

ETTA: Oh.

CLYDE: Oh. See? You don't even know where you're gonna be.

BURT: It's a sleeping room, jus' someplace t'sleep.

CLYDE: That means no visitors and suppose I want to visit?

ETTA (To BURT): Well, I'll probably be workin' in the movies.

BURT (Thinking): That's day work.

CLYDE (HE stares at BURT, then at ETTA): Oh shit...

ETTA: I can start anytime so there shouldn't be a problem...

BURT (Nods): Okay...

CLYDE: I see it now. I see the attraction.

ETTA: I imagine I'd be gone quite a bit...

CLYDE: Contract negotiations, celebrity luncheons.

BURT: My brother, Sherman, it's his house. He's a veteran
and he's blind but he can hear if you stay in the room.

CLYDE: Hey, wait a minute...you don't even know this guy or
his blind brother.

ETTA: Yeah and I don't know you...

CLYDE: We could fix that.

ETTA: What's your job?

CLYDE: My job?

ETTA (SHE looks him over): What do you get girls as they're
comin' off the train?

CLYDE: Get? I don't have to get! They come!

ETTA: Why is that?

CLYDE: Why do you think?

ETTA: They're stupid.

BURT: You wanna call?

ETTA: Yes, let's call. (SHE takes BURT's arm and moves away
from CLYDE)

CLYDE: Oh yes, let's call...

BURT: I could take you there after work. I'm off in about
thirteen minutes.

ETTA: That would be good. (Looks back at CLYDE) That would
be real good.

THEY exit. CLYDE stares after them, turns away.

CLYDE: What's my job...? Shit, where do these bitches come from?

Blackout.

Scene 2

BURT watches TV. ETTA wears a slip. SHE sets her hair with hot rollers. Beat.

ETTA: I think my throat is closing up. Those french fries were so dry, I think they're caught...like a lump in my throat. (SHE nudges BURT) I think those fries got caught in my throat.

BURT: Drink water.

ETTA: I wish I had a Coke. I saw this science experiment once, where they put this tooth in Coke, and over a period of a few weeks or days...or maybe it was just one day, it completely fell apart. Just disappeared.
I guess that could happen with a whole set of teeth if we were to sit around with a mouth full of Coca-Cola day and night. I wonder how it would work, the teeth comin' out, would you swallow and then what, would they come back in... somehow?
God, I'm stupid. What am I supposed to do? I thought by now I'd at least have some kinda extra work, somethin'...
I met this girl, Sheri, at the lunch counter? I thought she was pretty weird but she came out to be nice and she said that one way to break into movies is to have a videotape of yourself made.
Performing a scene with someone or maybe doin' a monologue. But the problem is, it cost. I wonder how I could get five hundred dollars?
I had four hundred, but that's just about gone. I wonder if I could find somebody with one of those video cameras you use at home?
(SHE nudges BURT, HE looks at her) Do you know anybody with a...home-movie camera?

BURT: I know people with video equipment.

ETTA: You do? Video! Yeah, that's what I need!

BURT: It's very expensive equipment, I don't think they'd let
  you just use it, just like that.

ETTA: I need an audition tape. (Beat) This is great, I'll
  brush up on my monologue or maybe get somebody to do a scene
  with me. When do you think you could... (SHE nudges him,
  HE turns) When do you think we could use the stuff.

BURT: What stuff?

ETTA: The videotape stuff.

BURT: I gotta ask.

ETTA: Do it.

BURT: I don't know.

ETTA: What do you mean?

BURT: This guy is not a very nice guy.

ETTA: Yeah.

BURT: He's a creep.

ETTA: What do you mean, a creep?

BURT (Beat): I don't really know.

ETTA (SHE touches him): You lie to me 'cause you think it's
  for my best good but all it does is make me not want to
  trust you. Don't lie to me, Burt. It makes me mad.

BURT: He's like, not a human being exactly.

ETTA: Go ask him.

BURT: He makes movies of women.

ETTA: Can you ask him now?

BURT: He's weird, Etta.

ETTA: I'll ask him.

BURT (HE looks away; beat): I'll ask him.

        SHE kicks him, HE looks up.

ETTA: Now. (HE stands) And while you're out...get me a
    Coke. Please. Okay? (Beat) Okay?!

       BURT moves upstage. The lights fade on ETTA.

Scene 3

       BEN is seated up left; HE looks like a man mutating
      into a wolf. DOLLY is standing downstage right of him
      with a drink; SHE faces front. BURT enters.

BEN (Beat): Dolly, could you make our guest a drink?

DOLLY (Exaggerated): You want a drink?

BURT: Well, if you're gonna have one...

DOLLY: I've got one.

BEN: Get his drink!

       DOLLY exits.

  What else?

BURT: Her name is Etta. She's got long arms and a big head.

BEN (Nods): A big-headed girl.

BURT: A natural blonde.

BEN: Personality, or no.

BURT (Beat): It's very difficult for me to say, because I
   can't hear. I can read her words, but since I can't hear
   how she says them, it's hard to say what she's like. You
   can tell a lot by how people sound, beyond what they tell
   you. If someone were to ask me, what's the worst part of
   losing my hearing, I'd have to tell them that it's not
   being able to hear if someone is sincere. Like with you for
   instance? I have never heard your voice and it's hard for
   me to know what kind of man you are.

BEN: I'm an asshole.

BURT: I guessed that.

BEN: I'm not ashamed, I'm not proud, but I don't try and put
     it on like I'm anything but an asshole.

BURT: I'd have to say...she could be anything.

BEN: Anything at all.

BURT: She spends hours making up. Even when there's no place
     to go. She likes to look her best.

BEN (HE stares after DOLLY): Vain. They are all vain, and
     then when they get old and they look like shit, they get
     pissed off! (Beat) So...she would like to be an actress?

BEN: She would like to be.

BEN: Is she any good?

BURT: I don't know. I do notice one thing. When she's
     talking, and she's excited, her face doesn't move. In my
     opinion, I'm not sure...that would make a very good actress.
     A wooden face.

BEN: Is she an easy lay?

BURT: Yes.

BEN: Details.

BURT: She came on to me the first night.

BEN: She came on to you?

BURT: She likes to have sex.

BEN: With a lot of white around the eyes?

BURT: Not at all.

BEN: She sounds like she has definite star quality.

BURT (Pause): How's Millie?

BEN: Millie...seems to have dropped out of sight.

BURT: Millie had star quality.

BEN: But she was unreliable.

BURT: She had a good sense of humor.

BEN: She was an addict.

BURT: After.

BEN (Cocks his head, shakes it): I don't know. I hate drugs
  myself. I don't even drink.

> DOLLY enters with two drinks.

  My wife is a drunk.

DOLLY: I didn't drink at all when you first met me.

BEN: So what? What's that supposed to mean? That I made you
  a boozebag?

DOLLY: Maybe.

BEN: That's shit! You just need a way to sit still. 'Cause
  if you stopped drinking you'd probably have to get up and
  live! And the pressure's too much! It's too damn much!
  Life scares the living shit out of you, and you're trying to
  blame me!

BURT (Facing away): I wish she wouldn't get involved with you,
  Ben...

BEN (To DOLLY): Oh Christ! you piss me off!!!

> Lights fade.

Scene 4

> THREE WOMEN stand downstage facing front. ETTA and
> SHERI are among them. A VOICE speaks to them from the
> dark.

VOICE: Hi. I'm the director, Thomas Schultz, and this is my
  A.D. Valerie. She'll be handling most of our problems and
  she'll be answering any questions you might have about your
  part.

> A FOURTH WOMAN enters.

Today we're casting for the role of the maid. It's a non-
speaking, nonpaying part, you'll plan to be here every
night for rehearsal and provide your own costume. It would

help if one of you were really a maid? (Beat) All right.
Who's first?

SHERI moves downstage.

SHERI: Hi Mr. Schultz, my name is Sheri Shineer and I'd like
to do a monologue from the musical Hair.

VOICE: That won't be necessary because you won't be talking.
The deal is, and I want to be as honest as I can with you
up-front, your type is not the type I had in mind.

SHERI: What type did you have in mind...?

VOICE: I don't know but you're not it...

SHERI: I am not my body...

VOICE: Maybe if you could all step up to the front of the
stage and...yes.

SHERI watches the remaining women move downstage.
SHE exits.

That's right. (Beat) Okay, you...second from the left,
what's your name?

ETTA: Uh...Lana?

VOICE: Don't you know?

ETTA: I'm changing it.

VOICE: Okay, the rest of you can go, thanks so much.

The OTHER GIRLS exit.

Have you ever worked in the theatre before, Lana?

ETTA: Oh yes I have, yes, I worked as an usherette for two-
and-a-half years at the Rialto...

VOICE: Wait a minute...

ETTA: Uh, Mr. Schlitz? Did I understand you to say that
nobody was gettin' paid here?

VOICE: Yes. We work for free. I mean, most of us work for
free, and some of us work for a token salary....Valerie?

ETTA: Well... (Chuckles) how can that be?

VOICE: Lana. This is Equity Waiver theatre, I told you at
the beginning the part was nonpaying.

ETTA: It took a minute to sink in.

VOICE: Yes well...

ETTA: I guess I could do it for the practice?

VOICE: Make up your mind.

ETTA: I haven't really worked in two months.

VOICE: That's not my problem.

ETTA: I used to work at the Thrifty lunch counter but I
burned my hand and they had to let me go and I was hopin'
to begin to pursue my professional career now that I was
between jobs.

VOICE: Do you want the part or not?

ETTA: No money at all?

VOICE: And you have to provide your own costume.

ETTA: Are you getting paid?

VOICE (Calling): Valerie?

ETTA: I really think I should have some money.

VOICE: The people producing this show can't afford to pay
everyone. I'm not making that much myself.

ETTA: Like how much do you make?

VOICE (Beat): I make ten dollars every night the show is up.

ETTA: Ten dollars? How do you live on ten dollars? You know
in a movie you get paid no matter if you're just standin'
around in the background...?

VOICE: Lana...

ETTA: It's evil not to pay people for work they do. That's
the time of their life.

VOICE: That's their choice.

ETTA: This can't be right. Man. I hate theatre.

> Lights fade out around ETTA. SHE remains lit. SHE
> turns as lights come up on SHERMAN and SHERI.

Scene 5

> SHERMAN is cleaning his M-16 at a kitchen table and
> listening to the ballgame. SHERI and ETTA enter and
> sit.

ETTA: Sherman.

SHERMAN: Home so early <u>again</u>, Etta?

ETTA: I don't know what to do. (Beat) I could take a job
typing. I'm a pretty bad typist.

SHERMAN: You'd improve.

SHERI: I hate office work.

ETTA: It makes me feel like I'm in a box.

SHERI: That's real.

ETTA: What would you do, Sherman?

SHERMAN: It doesn't matter. You and I have nothing in common.
What do you want to do?

ETTA: Be a movie star.

SHERMAN: What's that?

ETTA: You know, like...be an actress.

SHERMAN: And what's that?

SHERI: Sherman...?

SHERMAN: Like, what does <u>she</u> think it is?

ETTA: It's like...people are giving me money...'cause of who
I am.

SHERMAN: And who's that?

ETTA (Beat): I don't know.

SHERMAN: Maybe that's why you're not making much money.

ETTA: I'm not making anything.

SHERMAN: Maybe that's why. This is what stops most people,
not knowing who they are or where they fit in the marketplace.

ETTA: Where do you think I fit?

SHERMAN: Well, let me just say this. I imagine that you are
pretty, even when you lie or steal my cigarettes or when you
stay for days on end in a room I specifically told you was
for sleeping only! (SHERI and ETTA giggle silently) I
still _imagine_ you're a good-looking girl.

SHERI: She takes a good picture...

ETTA: You think so?

SHERI: Oh yeah, definitely.

SHERMAN: But that's not all, see what I'm saying?

SHERI: No.

SHERMAN: People can imagine what they want about her. Tabula
rasa.

SHERI: People can project what they want...

SHERMAN: She's like an archetype.

ETTA: Is that good?

SHERI: I think so. (Nods)

SHERMAN (Emphatic): No.

SHERI: Like Monroe? (Beat) Oh yeah.

SHERMAN: Icons who ascend to a level of worship and perish.
It's a cliché.

SHERI: Maybe you shouldn't be in the movies.

ETTA: It's my only dream, Sheri.

SHERMAN: You've had no interest?

ETTA: Burt has a friend. I don't know though, I don't know
about that. I'm supposed to go talk to him. But, I don't
know.

SHERI: He said she could make three hundred dollars a day.

SHERMAN: Burt's friend.

ETTA: Ben.

SHERMAN: Primordial ooze.

SHERI: He makes movies.

SHERMAN: Pornography.

SHERI: It's a service industry, Sherman.

ETTA: I could use a hundred dollars a day.

SHERMAN: Pornography in its focus on the genital experience
creates an ultimately carnal mind that is necessarily death-
oriented since the body is always in a progressive state of
decay. The earth begins to crawl up inside you...

SHERI: Ugh.

ETTA: We're dying anyway, who cares?

SHERMAN: The day you wake up with a mouth full of dirt, you'll
care.

SHERI: I don't think it's like that.

SHERMAN: You start thinking you're a body, you're not a body.

ETTA: Then why did I get a tattoo?

SHERMAN: It's macho.

SHERI: I got one when I first moved here, a snake on my
shoulder blade. I hate it.

SHERMAN: It made you feel like you had some control over your
life.

ETTA: I think I should have had something by now, don't you?
I mean, maybe this guy Ben is a break and I don't know it.
I mean, how _would_ I know it? I have never had a break. I
don't even know what a break looks like, do you?

SHERMAN: You can't know.

ETTA: Well, see there?

SHERI: I just do what's up next, and it seems to work out.

ETTA: And you know it could be these films are artistic.

SHERI: Yeah, Sherman.

SHERMAN: The difference between erotic art and Ben's business,
is the difference between gourmet dining and eating fifty
pounds of raw sewage in one sitting.

ETTA (Sneaking a cigarette): What do you think of the name
Lana, Sherman?

SHERMAN (HE catches her hand, takes the cigarette back): It
sounds like a fat girl trying to be thin.

SHERI (SHE lifts her skirt, flashes him): I bet he's not
really blind.

> SHERMAN slowly points his gun at SHERI, ETTA laughs.
> Blackout.

Scene 6

> BEN and SPENCER sit downstage. Lights flicker across
> their bodies. THEY are watching a movie. Pause.

SPENCER (Disgusted): I hate dogs.

BEN (Absorbed): How can you hate a dog? Dogs have some of the
best qualities of men.

SPENCER: How old is the girl in the doghouse?

BEN: Old enough...

SPENCER: How old?

BEN: These children are ancient sexual beings. They teach
me.

SPENCER: God...

BEN: Don't God me Spencer, I built the pyramids, don't use
that superior tone with me, I'm you.

SPENCER (Beat): Remember décolletage, Benjamin?

BEN: What's that supposed to mean?

SPENCER: A flash of thigh, a bare shoulder. Evening gowns,
Grace Kelly, a single strand of pearls. Teeth. A slight
overbite?

BEN (Sighs): God Spencer, you are so romantic.

        ETTA knocks and enters.

SPENCER (To ETTA): Welcome to the glue factory.

        SPENCER exits. BEN looks at ETTA.

BEN (Beat): I've heard very good things about you, high praise
from my friend Burt. He thinks you have talent. And after
meeting you, I have to admit, I'm impressed.

ETTA: Thank you.

BEN: I met Burt when I started out in this business but not
many people make it the way I have. Most lose their stuff,
like Burt, he couldn't handle the pressure.

ETTA: What pressure?

BEN: I personally don't know. Just, when people get out of
the business they say it's 'cause of the pressure.

ETTA: Burt thinks this is a mistake.

BEN: Burt thinks. Yes. Burt is a big star.

ETTA: He says it's the quickest way to ruin your chances.

BEN: I have footage on Burt. He's a lame dog.

ETTA: He never said anything about that.

BEN: Burt is a loser. I think you know that already. Am I
wrong? Okay. Good. Now, let's talk about you. I know you
want to make a short video, is that right?

ETTA: I want to make a tape of myself doing a monologue or a
scene so I can send it to casting directors or producers...

BEN: Okay. Back up. Has Burt told you I'm a producer?

ETTA: Not exactly.

BEN: I am. I make movies.

ETTA: Yeah, but...what kind?

BEN: Okay, let's not fool around. You know that.

ETTA: Yeah, I guess I do.

BEN: It's a business Etta. That's all it is. Business. And
I want to tell you one more thing here Etta. Maybe you know
this maybe you don't, but many of our finest stars made
their debut in a skinflick. Okay? That's number one.

ETTA: Like who?

BEN: I beg your pardon?

ETTA: Like what stars made their debut in a skinflick?

BEN: The world of cinema is like a secret society, Etta. I
myself would be happy to tell you the names of the other
members, but these stars, these very rich and influential
people consider discretion to be the first responsibility of
art. When and if you decide that this business opportunity
is one that suits your needs and if we find that you suit
ours, within a very short time these names will be as
familiar as your own. And believe me Etta, you will be
surprised and flattered to be among these elite, now where
was I, number two?

ETTA: Number two.

BEN: Number two, you could make a shitload of dough doin' one
film or maybe two films and use that money to start your
acting career. Use that to finance your audition tape
instead of coming in here and expecting me to bankroll your
ass for no reason whatsoever. Did you stop to ask yourself
that Etta? Why should I do this tape for you?

ETTA: I thought maybe as a favor.

BEN: I hate doing favors Etta, and you know why? Because in
the long run you will resent me. That's right, you should
always pay your way, Etta, and I'm speaking to you as a
friend would. Owe nobody!

ETTA: How much money could I make?

BEN: How much could you make. (Nods) I see. Cut to the
chase. Okay. Let's just say this. It depends.

ETTA: On what?

BEN: Well...we'd naturally have to talk about that. We'd
have to see.

ETTA: See what? See what I look like without my clothes?

BEN: That's not the only consideration.

ETTA: I look fine.

BEN: Show me.

ETTA (Beat): Just like that?

BEN: Exactly.

>   ETTA removes her blouse. Crossfade to KITTY. KITTY
> is facing upstage. SHE is nude from the waist up.

Scene 7

>   Lights come up on SHERI dipping a big sponge in a
> bucket of makeup and wiping down KITTY's back.

SHERI: Like my dad was dying of cirrhosis, okay? Depressed,
I mean, very. And he locked himself in his room with the
windows closed and the gas going full blast and like that
gas eats the oxygen in your body, so that when the cops
opened the door he exploded.

VOICE (Off): LANA?!

KITTY: That's sad.

SHERI: It was a mess more than a feeling, Kitty, he was
desperate. But like I started thinking about his...body
idea. Suppose you're not desperate, I mean, there should be
a way to scramble your protoplasm and...vamoose, you know?
I mean, it would be like building a car without doors, you
see what I'm saying?

>   ETTA enters wearing a robe and wig. SHE drops the
> wig on the floor.

KITTY: No.

VOICE (Off): YOU HAVE FIVE MINUTES LANA!

SHERI: I was just telling Kitty about disappearing the body.

ETTA: My hands smell like feet.

SHERI: I read about this yogi in India.

ETTA (SHE starts to sit down, grimaces): God, does anyone else have this infection...?

KITTY: It's a fungus, everybody has it.

SHERI: This yogi had mastered dematerialization to such a degree that he could vanish at will.

ETTA: Sheri will you shut up?

       KITTY and SHERI trade, KITTY wipes down SHERI.

SHERI: So like that information is in race memory, Kitty.

KITTY: What information?

ETTA: Dematerializing...

SHERI: That means, it's available to anyone, through the subconscious.

KITTY: I don't get it.

SHERI: 'Cause we are one mind.

KITTY: What's the point of being able to disappear, anyway?

SHERI: You're walking down the street and a man comes out of nowhere waving a gun....He feels like he's dead inside, misery loves company, he sees you. What happens?

KITTY: Get shot.

ETTA: Dematerialize, Kitty.

KITTY: I never heard of that happening.

SHERI: I'm just saying we should have that option.

ETTA: You know, I used to really enjoy sex? (Beat) Now every time I make love even if it's somebody I like I get this terrible urge that seems to come out of nowhere and it's all I can do to keep from gouging his eyes out or slitting his throat...

KITTY: Or hitting him over the head with a crystal ashtray
you had to work two days to pay for.

ETTA (Curious): Yeah, yeah...what is that?

KITTY (Pause; thoughtfully): It's like some kind of rage.

SHERI: I'm not angry.

KITTY: Me either.

ETTA: I don't think I'm angry.

VOICE (Off): LANA?! WHERE'S LANA?

ETTA: Shit...

VOICE: LANA!!!?

ETTA: I AM NOT (Standing slowly as SHE speaks) WEARING THAT
STINKING COSTUME, YOU STUPID SON OF A BITCH. WHERE'S BEN!!!!

    ETTA exits. THEY watch her.

KITTY (Beat): She hasn't been in the business very long to
complain about a dirty rig.

    Crossfade to BURT.

Scene 8

    BURT sits alone watching TV. A suitcase is near his
feet. Clothes are being flung into it from the shadows.
ETTA enters a moment later. SHE's packing.

BURT: He's married.

ETTA: Grow up.

BURT: What happened to just doing one film?

ETTA: What about it?

BURT: I thought that was the idea.

ETTA: What's your idea, Burt?

BURT: I don't know.

ETTA: If you don't have any ideas, you can't play.

BURT: What are you mad at me for?

ETTA: You can't be me and make my decisions.

BURT: I don't know what you're talking about.

ETTA: It's degrading.

BURT: What does that mean?

ETTA: You can't be anything to me, you can't be me, you can't do anything for me, what is it you want?

BURT: I don't want you to go.

ETTA: If I keep working like this, I'll make more money than my lawyer.

BURT: Well, is that the point? Money?

ETTA: Yes.

BURT: I think the point is not to screw your life up.

ETTA: Are you in love with me?

BURT: I used to think I was.

ETTA: Okay, so what do you want to have happen?

BURT: Get married?

ETTA: Oh, get married.

BURT: Yes.

ETTA: And what? Have a kid, have a child?

BURT: I like kids, I mean...yeah, kids would be fine by me.

ETTA: Right, kids...and what else? A house?!

BURT: Yes, yes!

ETTA: Jesus!

BURT: What?

ETTA: I don't want that, that's not what I want. House,
kids, husband, prison, <u>National Inquirer</u>, sour milk, cheese
every day, it makes me feel sick!

BURT: Marriage is a woman's destiny.

ETTA: What?

BURT: Nothing.

ETTA: If something is your destiny, it shouldn't make you
feel like puking your guts out!!

BURT: What about our sex? What about that?

ETTA: I hate sex.

BURT: Our sex is a commingling of spirits. It's the kind of
sex married people have, Etta.

ETTA: I can have sex with anything and make it look like I
enjoy it. I'm a pro.

BURT: You're just being mean now. You're just trying to make
me feel bad for complaining. All right. You don't want to
be with me. Okay. But you know it's not a good idea to do
things for money, money is never good motivation. It turns
you hard.

ETTA: I don't do it for the money.

BURT: Are you on something?

ETTA: No!

BURT: 'Cause my brother hates drugs. He'd shit if he thought
you were on something...

ETTA: Did you hear what I said?

BURT: You don't do it for the money. (Beat) You don't?

ETTA: No.

BURT: What for then?

ETTA: I'm good at it.

BURT: Etta. That's disgusting.

ETTA: What's disgusting?

BURT: Don't you think I know what you're talking about?

ETTA: No, I don't think you do.

BURT: I've seen those movies, Etta.

ETTA: What am I talking about?

BURT: Screwing.

ETTA: What I'm talking about, Burt, is business.

BURT: Bullshit.

ETTA: Have it your way.

BURT: What about it do you like?

ETTA: I want to thank you for all the help you've given me, Burt, I really appreciate it.

BURT: What do you think, you can just brush me off, just kiss me off, just like that?! You think you need an excuse to be a whore, you don't need an excuse. Money, no money, good, no good, I don't know what you're talking about anymore, I can't see into your face, how you're talking to me...it doesn't respect anything, Etta. I could be something to you. I could. But you won't have it.

> HE sits down, rubs his ears. Pause. SHE takes a box out of her valise. SHE nudges him with the box.

ETTA: It's a gift. (Beat) It's a white silk shirt.

BURT: Where am I supposed to wear this, the Academy Awards?

ETTA: Goodbye, Burt. (SHE takes the TV, crosses away from him)

BURT: WHY CAN'T YOU JUST TELL ME WHAT IT DOES FOR YOU??!

ETTA (Stops; beat): It makes me feel like I'm really here.

BURT: But what about me. (HE turns away)

> ETTA exits.

When you leave, where will I be? Who's going to see me? Sherman can't see me. My job can't see me. Somebody needs to see me for me to be okay, I can't say I'm gonna be okay if I don't have that, Etta!

Lights fade out on BURT.

<u>Scene 9</u>

A beach in Cancun, Mexico. Beach sounds are heard.
A light comes up on BEN. HE is lying on a reclining
lounge chair in Speedos and sunglasses. ETTA sits
beside him sipping a drink; SHE wears a caftan. SHE
watches him a long beat.

ETTA: You have so many moles, Ben. Aren't you worried about
getting skin cancer?

BEN: I can't <u>stop</u> thinking about it.

ETTA: You should wear sunscreen.

BEN (Beat): I'm trying to remember the color of the room I
grew up in. (Beat) I think it was...blue. (Pause) My bed
was under a window, I would leave the shade up, moonlight
made the walls of my room look white. Sometimes I would
wake up, and there he would be, sitting on the edge of my
bed, staring at me...and I would ask him...what was wrong.
But he'd just sit there, and stare, and not say a word.
(Beat) He was a drunk.

ETTA: Who?

BEN: My father.

ETTA (Beat): My dad and my mom's dad were the same person.

BEN (Sits up, slowly turns): Are you shittin' me?

ETTA: No...

BEN: That's freakish. (Still staring) Aren't you supposed
to be dead?

ETTA: No.

BEN: It's a good thing you're not going to have a baby.

ETTA: Yeah.

BEN: It'd be a turnip.

HE lies back down. Pause.

ETTA: He used to wrap himself up in a blanket and chase me
around the house. One day my mom saw that and started
screaming at him. And right after that we moved. We didn't
see him again for a long time and then one day he showed up.
We were watching the moonshot and he came to the screen door
and looked in. I unlocked the door and he came in and the
three of us sat there without speaking, watching this guy
walk on the moon, till finally...he just got up and left. I
looked at my mom but she wouldn't look at me. I told her
she should go out and say goodbye but she wouldn't answer.
She was always quiet but she hardly ever spoke after that.
(Beat. SHE sits up, takes off her glasses) I don't like
Mexico, Ben, it's too hot. I want to go home.

BEN: Go.

ETTA: What about you?

BEN: I made some bad deals. Spencer wants to pay me back.
Screw him.

ETTA: You're not going back.

BEN: Correctamente bien.

ETTA: What about me?

BEN: Screw you.

        HE laughs a short convulsive laugh. ETTA watches
    him. SHE remains lit, as the lights fade on BEN and
    the beach.

                        Scene 10

        A dance hall. Music comes up: "Red Roses for a Blue
    Lady." A COUPLE dance in a spotlight. The WOMAN looks
    at her watch, puts her hand out, the MAN gives her some
    tickets, THEY exit. ETTA and SHERI enter, dancing
    together.

ETTA: So we were just talking in the bar and at one point he
said, you have such a cruel smile. Cruel smile, right? So
then I knew. I take him upstairs, I tie him up with his own

necktie, I step on his hand and I call him Dog. So then he
gives me plane fare home, his Spanish language edition of
Spanker's Monthly and he's very clean. Japanese.

SHERI: I've always wanted a stranger to ask for my autograph.

ETTA: He wasn't seeing me, he was seeing Lana, in a leather
corset.

SHERI: It got you home, I have friends who've never come back
from Mexico.

ETTA: Anything can happen there, it's so poor.

SHERI: So many miracles occur in Third World countries....I
think that poverty inspires a greater belief in the
supernatural.

ETTA: Speaking of supernatural, look at this guy coming in.

SHERI: Psycho.

ETTA: His name is Dwight.

SHERI: Dwight, like Norman? Strictly from the Bates Motel.

ETTA: He seems like he's got a lot of money.

SHERI: He's a good-looking white guy. He could date anybody.
I mean. Except for his eyes...he's handsome.

ETTA: He has a funny arm.

SHERI: Look at his shoes, patent-leather evening pumps, two
hundred and sixty dollars. He's wearing an eight-hundred-
dollar suit. You have to ask yourself, what's this guy
doing paying you twenty-five cents a minute to dance.

ETTA: He talks.

SHERI: To talk then.

ETTA: He seems like he's lonely.

SHERI: They're always lonely. It's because all their friends
are dead. Oh here comes my dreamboat. He's looking for me.
He's waving. (SHE waves) 'Ola, Carlos! (Quietly) You fat
pig. See you later...

    SHERI moves off, DWIGHT enters.

DWIGHT: Hello there, Lana.

ETTA: Hi, Dwight.

DWIGHT: Business is slow tonight.

ETTA: Yeah.

DWIGHT: You're looking especially pretty this evening.

ETTA: This is the same dress I always wear.

DWIGHT (Beat; HE sighs): I would like it if you wouldn't use
   that tone of voice when you accept a compliment. As if I
   was insulting your intelligence.

ETTA: Well?

DWIGHT: If I think you look nice I say so. That's all.

ETTA: You want to dance?

DWIGHT: Not really.

ETTA: I have to take your tickets even if we just talk.

DWIGHT: I came over to ask you if you'd like to go out with
   me. Since it's a slow night, maybe they'll let you off. We
   could go someplace.

ETTA: Like where?

DWIGHT: Ladies' choice.

ETTA: The health department closed the coffee shop, if that's
   what you're talking about.

DWIGHT: No. I was thinking we could have dinner someplace, a
   nice place, then maybe...

ETTA: We could stop off at your house.

DWIGHT: My mother's away for a few days. I'd like to show
   you our collection of porcelain figurines. There's one that
   looks just like you.

ETTA (Beat; SHE looks away): I don't think so.

DWIGHT: Why not?

         JAMES appears upstage. HE lights a cigarette before
      making his way over.

ETTA: I don't date the customers.

DWIGHT: I thought by now we were friends.

ETTA: The manager is watching us, you'll have to give me some
tickets.

JAMES (To ETTA):   Hi ugly.

ETTA: What are you doin' here, James?

JAMES: Spencer's been lookin' for you.

ETTA: So what?

JAMES: So he wants to see you.

ETTA: What for?

JAMES: How should I know.   (To DWIGHT)   What are you lookin'
at?

DWIGHT: Nothing.

JAMES: What are you tryin' to date my sister here?

DWIGHT: We were talking about having some dinner, yes.

JAMES: Oh, some dinner? I see, dinner. Are you eating these
days Etta?

ETTA: Get lost.

JAMES (To DWIGHT):   I think she wants you to get lost.

ETTA: Not him...

JAMES: This is a strange place to find a girlfriend, pal, you
plug one of these and your dick falls off...

ETTA: I'm calling the manager.

JAMES (To DWIGHT, grimacing):   What's wrong with your arm?!

ETTA: You're an asshole...

DWIGHT: I had a muscle disease as a child.

JAMES: So now you're gimpified, is that right?

ETTA: Get the fuck out of here!

JAMES: Must have been something I said, shit, I'm such a
jerk.

>   SHERI enters as JAMES starts to leave.

Hi Sheri...how you doin'? What time you off?

SHERI: 2:00.

JAMES: Maybe I'll let you read my cards?

SHERI: I can't wait.

JAMES: We'll see you tomorrow, Etta.

>   JAMES exits. SHERI exits in the opposite direction.

ETTA (Thinking, SHE shakes her head): Great!

>   DWIGHT takes her arm, squeezes; SHE pulls away, HE
>   holds on. THEY freeze.

DWIGHT: What about if I pay you?

>   Blackout.

Scene 11

>   The lights come up on SPENCER as HE watches JAMES
>   light a cigarette.

SPENCER (Beat): <u>Gone</u>! Just like that, just like that! Shit.

JAMES: If you're so sensitive maybe you should get out of the
business.

SPENCER: You make me sick. You know that? You sicken me!

>   A knock on the door. BOTH MEN watch the door. The
>   knock comes again.

Try and keep your mouth shut.

JAMES: Come in.

>   SPENCER glares at JAMES, ETTA enters. A bandage
>   covers her left eye, her right cheek is bruised, her
>   arm is in a sling.

SPENCER: Good to see you, Etta. (Beat) You're looking well.

ETTA: I feel good.

SPENCER: Did you fall down a manhole?

JAMES: She's been bangin' freaks two at a time and she's getting what she deserves, isn't that right?

SPENCER: Shut up.

ETTA: Spencer. If the question is Ben, I have no idea where he is. He left me in Cancun with five hundred pesos and I haven't seen him since.

SPENCER: Ben is too slimy not to leave a trail, Etta. Ben is handled. (JAMES begins to laugh) James doesn't know why he's laughing. Do you?

JAMES: I think something's funny.

SPENCER: And he can't shut up, can you?

JAMES: Why should I?

SPENCER (Beat; HE turns back to ETTA): What are you doing for work these days, Etta?

ETTA: I work at a dance place.

SPENCER: Like Arthur Murray?

> JAMES laughs; ETTA laughs a beat later.

ETTA: Like taxi dancers.

JAMES: Like hookers dancing with scumballs...

ETTA: James is a regular.

JAMES: Eat shit.

SPENCER: So you're making a living wage?

ETTA: I do all right. I work part time and I go to school. (JAMES laughs) I'm taking a class in court reporting... (JAMES laughs harder. To JAMES) Screw you!

SPENCER: Etta, I have a little business proposition for you. Do you know what a talent scout is?

ETTA: Yes.

SPENCER: It's self-evident.

ETTA: It's somebody that scouts talent.

JAMES: Brilliant.

SPENCER: You come into contact with a lot of young women.
  They are needy...they need things...money, a job, a place,
  but mostly they need money.

ETTA: Oh brother...

SPENCER: Maybe movies wouldn't be an option but you present
  it in such a way as to persuade...

ETTA: For Ben's business?

JAMES: No, for MGM.

SPENCER: It's not Ben's business anymore. It's mine and I'm
  asking you to come in as talent coordinator.

ETTA: What's that?

JAMES: It's a hawk, idiot head.

SPENCER: You've made movies.

ETTA: That's right.

SPENCER: I want to make better movies.

ETTA: You want a class movie with class action.

SPENCER: I knew she was smart.

JAMES: Shit.

ETTA: Good-looking women with no problems, no junkies, no
  freaks, and they want to make a pornographic movie that has
  the potential of coming back at them years from now when
  they want to marry a minister or run for Supreme Court.

SPENCER: This is business, Etta.

ETTA: I don't want to hustle anybody.

SPENCER: You don't have to, the dollar sign is the bottom
  line. Better pay, better working conditions equal better
  product, it's a whole different operation.

JAMES: You are making a big mistake here, Spencer.

SPENCER: Shut up!

JAMES (To ETTA): Stupid.

ETTA: Why don't you go home and eat a cockroach.

JAMES: I don't do that anymore!

SPENCER: James had this job, isn't that right, James? (JAMES
   looks away) But James cannot keep track of the women. They
   vanish, sometimes the day of shooting, sometimes in the
   middle of a film, or one or two movies later. You never
   know what becomes of them, they just disappear!

JAMES: Screw you.

SPENCER: Screw you! (JAMES moves away) So. I am prepared
   to pay you three a week and fifty for every warm body you
   scare up. There's the deal.

ETTA: Is that what James was making?

JAMES: No way, bitch... (To SPENCER) Can you feature this?

ETTA: You want me to do a better job than James and you want
   to pay me less.

SPENCER: I'll pay you four a week and a hundred for every
   girl that completes an assignment.

JAMES: You're pissing me off, Spencer.

SPENCER: Why don't you get lost for a while.

        JAMES and SPENCER exchange looks; JAMES looks at
        ETTA.

JAMES: Yeah, okay. (Laughing, HE exits)

SPENCER: James is walking out to his car right now imagining
   that you and I are having it off. (Sighs) James is a
   victim of this business. When he's not dreaming of latex
   miniskirts he's sitting in a quarter booth. Images of
   comfort and security. (HE pulls three hundred dollars from
   his wallet) One week's salary.

        ETTA starts to take the money, stops, moves away.

ETTA (Beat): I don't think so, Spencer. (SHE gathers her
   things to leave)

SPENCER: It's really not about thinking, Etta, it's about
instinct, survival of the fittest, adaptation to
environmental demands. Many women don't like business, they
find it dull, or too competitive, or their priorities shift
and they lose interest, but I don't think you're that kind
of woman.

ETTA: What kind?

SPENCER: You ever been married?

ETTA: Once. (Beat) Look Spencer, the deal is I'm gonna take
acting classes and get my SAG card. I mean that's why I
came out here and with court reporting I mean it pays real
well and you can work around auditions so...

SPENCER: You know, Etta, not everyone is Grace Kelly.

ETTA: Nobody is, Spencer, she's dead.

SPENCER: What I'm trying to tell you is, you're no actress, I
think we both know that.

ETTA: Well, I'm better than I was.

SPENCER: But you're not good enough to overcome having done
skinflicks.

ETTA: Overcome.

SPENCER: Yes.

ETTA (Beat): Ben said a lot of stars did movies to finance
their careers.

SPENCER: He lied.

ETTA: Ben said that since they all did it, it was acceptable,
and that nobody thought anything about it.

SPENCER: What world do you live in, Etta? (Beat) What do
you think, legitimate actors and actresses risk their
credibility to make porno, for what? For money? You meet
actors waiting tables, tending bar, they could make better
money here, why don't they?

ETTA (Beat): 'Cause it ruins your chances?

SPENCER: 'Cause people are hypocrites, Etta. If you and
another actress are up for the part of the Virgin Mary and
both of you are equally awful, who do you think they're
going to give it to? You? With your spread shots from here

to Timbuktu. It's a high-profile industry, somebody is
bound to recognize you. Especially with your circulation.
You're a star.

ETTA (Pause): It's my only dream, Spencer.

SPENCER: Dreams are a lot like movies, they function to keep
you from seeing how shitty life is. But once you know that,
you're free of those stupid expectations that drive people
crazy.

ETTA: I feel like somebody slipped the bones out of my body.
(Pause) I don't know what I'm supposed to want if I don't
want that, I mean, if I can't have that, what am I supposed
to want?

SPENCER: Money is a good place to start, you have a little
feeling for it, otherwise you would never have made your
first reel, am I wrong?

ETTA: No.

SPENCER: Think about buying a fur coat and a closet to put it
in...think about a car the color of your eyes built in the
country your ancestors came from. Think about getting into
that car and driving home to visit those people who checked
their ambition years ago. You're still gonna be in the
movies, Etta.

ETTA: My friend Sherman says that the way to get what you
want is to keep a picture of it in your heart. That any
image you can hold on to, you can make it happen in your
life.

SPENCER (Beat): You go to the movies?

ETTA: I haven't been going much lately.

SPENCER: When you imagine yourself up there on the wide
screen, with the big stars, what do you see?

ETTA: When?

SPENCER: In your head, in your heart, in your imagination,
think. People are sitting in the dark, eating popcorn,
watching you, what do they see?

    ETTA takes a long beat to see what SHE actually
    thinks.

ETTA: Lana. They see Lana. Her body makeup streaked with
sweat 'cause she's running a temperature from an infection

she can't seem to get rid of. She's smiling at a man she
hates, and giving herself to him, 'cause it's what he wants.
It's what everybody in the audience wants.

SPENCER: And what does she want?

ETTA (Beat): Bigger tits.

SPENCER: And what do you want?

       Pause. SHE looks at him, holds out her hand.

ETTA: A raise.

       Beat. Blackout.

Scene 12

       Music. Lights up on the dance hall. SHERI is
standing downstage looking front. JAMES enters. HE
lights a cigarette before crossing to her.

SHERI: Do you have to smoke so much? Christ...!

JAMES: How you doin' Sheri? (SHE turns away) What? Are you
mad about the other night? I had to work.

SHERI: Yeah...

JAMES: So it's all the same, right? We both made money,
except you came here.

SHERI: I came here, what's that supposed to mean?

JAMES: Just that you came here and picked up a few bucks,
right?

SHERI: Yeah.

JAMES: I bet you can barely get high on what you make here.

SHERI: I'm not getting high like I used to. I'm changed.

JAMES: All I'm saying is you could do better.

SHERI (Beat): So, what are you doin' later on?

JAMES: I have some people I gotta see.

SHERI: Business again?

JAMES: For people like us, business is ninety percent of our lives.

SHERI: You and I are not the same kind of people, James.

JAMES: Well anyway, my business involves one other person.

SHERI: I'm not loaning you any money.

JAMES: Sheri, you are so paranoid.

SHERI: I am not a savings and loan.

JAMES: And here it is, I used to get you high...

SHERI: Please...that shit you <u>sold</u> me?

JAMES: I just thought you might want to make some easy money, that's all.

SHERI: Nothing you do is easy, James, that's you.

JAMES: That's me, what's that supposed to mean?

SHERI: How much?

JAMES: Five big ones.

SHERI: What's a big one to you, James, a buck?

JAMES: A hundred is a big one, and five big ones is five hundred dollars.

SHERI: Who do I have to kill?

JAMES: God, you know, you really have a good sense of humor?

SHERI: Eat me.

JAMES: Seriously, like...Joan Rivers.

SHERI: What's the deal?

JAMES: It's a movie.

SHERI: Why are they paying so much?

JAMES: Part of it's travel money.

SHERI: Where do I have to go, Mars?

JAMES (Laughs): Uranus.

SHERI: Where do I have to go?!

JAMES: Mexico.

SHERI: Mexico? (Uncertain) No, (Firm) no, forget it.

JAMES: Forget five hundred dollars?

SHERI: Don't you think I know what kind of movie they make
in Mexico?

JAMES: What kind?

SHERI: You know.

JAMES: No, I'm stupid, you're smart. You tell me.

SHERI (Beat): You have to do it with a donkey.

JAMES (Bursts out laughing): Donkey?! (Laughs again) I'm so
sure! (Calms down) You don't have to do it with a donkey.
No.

SHERI: So then what do I have to do?

JAMES: Although, it's not a bad idea.

SHERI: James...!

JAMES: Lay there and cooperate.

SHERI: Five hundred dollars.

JAMES: And I can get you high.

SHERI: Straight sex.

JAMES: And I'm driving your ass down there, we have a party
in the car, I got some smack, some blow, I got a bottle of
Chivas and some whites if we need them.

SHERI: Five hundred dollars.

JAMES: You wear some rubber is all.

SHERI: That's not straight sex!

JAMES (Surprised): It's not?

SHERI: No!

JAMES (Beat): Okay, screw it, I'll catch you later.

SHERI: Hey! (Pause) Are you going to be there or what?

JAMES: Yes I am.

SHERI: 'Cause like I wouldn't mind a trip to Mexico but like
I don't want to get stranded, you know?

JAMES (Smiles): What do you think, I'm gonna leave your ass
in Mexico, I'm so sure.

      THEY freeze. Blackout.

Scene 13

     Lights up on KITTY and ETTA seated in the office.
ETTA is well-dressed, upscale, in a business suit.

ETTA: So tell me Kitty, how's Moe?

KITTY: Moe's good, yeah...he's real good. He's been clean
like, what, three weeks?

ETTA: Three weeks.

KITTY: Pretty clean. Chipping on the weekends is all.
Recreational. (Beat) So what do you think, Etta?

ETTA: Let me see.

     KITTY stands. SHE is pregnant.

KITTY: I wouldn't want anything to happen to the baby.

ETTA: It's not a baby yet.

KITTY: Moe wanted me to get rid of it.

ETTA: Moe is not as stupid as he looks.

KITTY: I'm two months.

ETTA: You look four.

KITTY: I can't remember.

ETTA: Okay Kitty, look. I have a good doctor in Century City, a thousand dollars.

KITTY: A thousand dollars.

ETTA: You could make that in two days, plus five hundred extra 'cause you're pregnant.

KITTY: Five hundred extra.

ETTA: And you still have time to get rid of your problem.

KITTY: It's not a problem.

ETTA: It's going to be.

KITTY: You don't like kids.

ETTA: Don't pretend to know anything. What are you, twelve years old? You know something, you don't know shit.

KITTY: I know you don't like kids.

ETTA: I have a kid. She lives with people she calls Mom and Dad and when she gets sick she goes to a doctor and when she needs discipline she will understand why she's being punished. The element of random violence will not be present in her life.

KITTY: I want to keep my baby.

ETTA: And teach it what? How to be you, how to be Moe?

KITTY: What's wrong with Moe?

ETTA: Kitty, I'm sure you've noticed how a baby can scream? Did you know they're supposed to be allowed to do that? It's good for them? Because they're pissed off. They're pissed off about being in the world, and so they scream.

KITTY (Pause): One time, I saw Moe rip a faucet out of a wall when he couldn't get it to stop dripping. He hates noise.

      KITTY gets a cigarette out of her bag; ETTA lights it for her.

ETTA: Sheri used to work for Moe.

KITTY: Sheri did?

ETTA: She popped, he had her back on the street in two weeks.

KITTY: Moe said I didn't have to work anymore.

ETTA: That's what he told Sheri.

KITTY: I didn't know Sheri had a kid.

ETTA: She doesn't. He's a memory.

KITTY (Beat): I don't believe you.

ETTA (Holds the phone out): Call Sheri, ask her.

> JAMES enters. HE's nervous, smoking. HE sits down, stares away from the women.

KITTY: No.

ETTA: It's a simple solution to a complex problem, Kitty, think about it and let me know today.

KITTY: I'm gonna see Moe and see what he says. 'Cause like, he seems happy about the baby and everything and I could see a baby making a big difference in our lives, a good difference, you know? We'd have a reason to get straight? For the sake of the baby? I'll call you, Etta, okay? I'll call you. (To JAMES) Bye, Bug.

JAMES: Bitch.

> KITTY exits. JAMES lights a cigarette from one in the ashtray. ETTA makes a phone call.

JAMES: Isn't it fucked how sometimes you want things to work out a certain way but they never do, they just keep...you know, screwing up and I wonder, like, do you think that's genetic?

ETTA: Shut up.

JAMES: Like with me and Dixie. We were gonna get married and like have a house, this and that.

ETTA: But you had to kill your parents.

JAMES: Just my mother. (Beat) She made me kill her.

ETTA (SHE hangs up): Have you seen Sheri?

JAMES: WHAT DO I LOOK LIKE, PUBLIC INFORMATION, HOW SHOULD I KNOW WHERE SHE IS??

ETTA: Stop yelling.

JAMES: My parole officer says that every time a person
commits a crime it's because they're reaching for a better
life. What do you think? Do you think that's evolution
expressing itself?

ETTA: Why don't you take a bath once in a while?

JAMES: You got any money, Etta?

ETTA: This is a loan...do you know what a loan is? (SHE
digs in her purse, hands him twenty dollars)

JAMES: What am I supposed to do with twenty dollars? I can't
even get laid for twenty dollars. I mean I could, not that
I ever pay for it...I mean, I like to pay for it 'cause...
you know...you can do what you want...but not for twenty
dollars Etta, I need at least fifty.

ETTA: I'm not giving you fifty dollars to get laid.

JAMES has two cigarettes going; HE lights a third.

JAMES: How about you and me go someplace for a drink?

ETTA: No.

JAMES: You think you're too good to go out with me?

ETTA: Yes.

JAMES: Don't you think I know that? I'm offering to buy you
a drink, I'd like to buy you dinner but I'm short, I mean,
I'm not short, I'm average height for a man with my build,
but I look that way 'cause I work out.

ETTA: What are you on?

JAMES: Speed.

ETTA: You're talking like a jerk.

JAMES: Etta, I take it every day, it helps me think.

ETTA (SHE pulls more money from her purse and hands it to
him): Here. Now get lost.

JAMES (HE looks at it; beat): I don't want to go home right
now. I don't really feel like being by myself and I don't
feel like being with strangers and you and Spencer are the

only friends I have. You don't have to loan me any money,
here... (HE lays the money on the desk; HE takes a chair,
straddles it) You don't even have to go out in public with
me, I'll just sit here awhile, I won't talk. If I could
just stay here for a while I think I could be okay, if I
could just get my breath, and cool out I won't even talk and
you can just do your work. Okay? Okay?

> Pause. ETTA watches JAMES. HE lays his arms across
> the back of the chair and puts his head on his arms.
> Light change. ETTA moves around her desk, SPENCER
> enters. THEY watch JAMES.

Scene 14

JAMES (Explodes): YOU ARE NOT MY BOSS!!

ETTA: I've been waiting a long time for this talk, James.

JAMES: Sheri could have been gone for months without a soul
in the world being any the wiser except for you now have to
be the big eye.

ETTA: I love this, it's my fault, right?

JAMES: Yes! Because women don't belong in business.

ETTA: Did you know she was expected for dinner?

JAMES: How would I?

ETTA: Sunday night?

JAMES: Oh Christ, Spencer...!

ETTA: Her mother called me.

JAMES: So what?!

ETTA: She said Sheri left town with you.

JAMES: She's lying.

ETTA: She also said she called the police and they might be
showing up pretty soon...

SPENCER: What happened, James?

JAMES: How should I know...?

SPENCER: James?!

JAMES: I DON'T KNOW!

ETTA (Kinder): You know something, James.

JAMES (Beat): I heard...don't ask me where, that somebody
thinks she might have gone to Mexico to do a movie.

ETTA: Mexico.

SPENCER: Oh shit.

ETTA: What in the hell did you take her down there for?!

JAMES: I don't know!

ETTA (Rage): GOD DAMN YOU, I KNEW HER.

JAMES (Cowed): So you knew her? Big deal. Know somebody, it
makes a difference.

ETTA: She was my friend!

JAMES: She was my friend too...I don't know what happened,
she was supposed to meet me and I waited and waited and
finally I just said...fuck it. What am I supposed to do
Spencer, (Giggles) hang around, waiting for a...a...woman?

SPENCER: Where did you take her?

JAMES: Just a house.

SPENCER: JAMES!

JAMES: I took her to Ben.

SPENCER: Ben.

ETTA: I didn't know he was doing business.

JAMES: I dropped her off, she wanted to go. She asked me for
a ride, that's all.

SPENCER: And then what?

JAMES: I went back to pick her up. Nobody was there, the
house was empty. Nothing.

ETTA: Did you call Ben...?

JAMES: I don't where he is.

ETTA: Bullshit!

JAMES: I don't know, he calls me, that's all...I never know
  where he is.

SPENCER: You haven't talked to him since?

JAMES (Beat): Once.

SPENCER: And what did he say?!

JAMES: He says she disappeared.

ETTA: You mean like vanished?

JAMES: Like that's all he said!!

ETTA: He's lying!

SPENCER: I think you should vanish as well.

JAMES: Absolutely...

SPENCER (HE hands him some money): Now.

ETTA: We're just gonna let him go?

JAMES: I can't split without my stash.

SPENCER: If you are determined to risk it, fine.

JAMES: Risk what?

ETTA: Spencer!

SPENCER: If you want to stay outside, I assume you do.

JAMES: You would give me up.

SPENCER: In a nanosecond.

ETTA: Shit!

SPENCER (To JAMES): What are you waiting for?

JAMES (Astonished): This is my home, all my friends are here.
  How long do I have to stay gone?

SPENCER: Forever.

JAMES: Is that necessary?

SPENCER: Get out of here you scum-sucking leech before I put the police on you myself.

JAMES (Beat; to ETTA): I'll get you for this. (HE exits)

SPENCER (Pause): Etta.

ETTA: Don't say it.

SPENCER: Sheri was a big girl, she knew what she was doing.

ETTA: Spencer...?

SPENCER: I didn't kill her. (SHE stares at him a beat) What do you want to do, get mad?

ETTA: I want to get even.

SPENCER: Oh shit, Etta, grow up.

> HE moves off, ETTA looks front. SHE remains lit while the lights fade around her. SHE moves downstage. A light comes up on DOLLY.

Scene 15

> DOLLY is wearing a loose wrapper; SHE holds a drink in one hand and a fan in the other. SHE's drunk.

ETTA: You hear about Sheri?

DOLLY: Oh Christ, is that what you came to talk about?

ETTA: I want to know where Ben is, Dolly.

DOLLY: Like, what? I'm supposed to help you? Screw off, Etta.

ETTA: What's the matter, Dolly, you getting old?

DOLLY: Maybe I think about the past a lot, things that happened, things that didn't work out. But I hold a grudge for you. Maybe that's not right, but I do.

ETTA: About Ben.

DOLLY: Ben and me had a good thing going.

ETTA: Ben was chewing you up and spitting you out a piece at
    a time.

DOLLY: Well...it was good in the beginning.

ETTA: Everything is good in the beginning. It's only when
    they start to change, when their repulsive personal habits
    start to show up, that you have to wonder what you were
    thinking in the first place.

DOLLY: Yeah, we all change, but I don't like the way you've
    changed, so get out.

ETTA: They ever find your sister, Dolly?

DOLLY: Shut up...

ETTA: She was dating James for a while, and then all of a
    sudden she was nowhere to be found.

DOLLY (Beat): Ben says she's in Texas...but...I don't think
    she's anywhere, you know...I just have that feeling. I can
    always tell when he's lying, that son of a bitch.
        You know, in my business, you would have thought I'd meet
    a lot of men and that one of them would have meant something
    to me... (Beat) I get lonely, I brood. It's probably
    because of this that Ben begins to look good.
        I went down to see him a few months ago. To see, you know,
    if there was anything there. He wanted it too. (Beat) I
    couldn't recognize him. I'm Mexican and in Mexico, I'm very
    psychic. When he met me at the airport and kissed me hello,
    I got this taste of dirt in my mouth.
        He hugged me, I heard my bones crack and turn to dust and
    I saw us become this cloud of white powder blowing down the
    runway. I took a plane out of there so fast.
        He's in Mexico City, Etta, he has a house near
    Chapultapec Park, he does business out of the hotel there.
    But don't go yourself. Send a man. I know somebody. I'll
    give you his name.

        Lights fade.

Scene 16

Lights come up on MAX. HE sits downstage at a small table. ALEC sits upstage on a bar stool. ETTA moves to MAX. Bar sounds come up. SHE takes check from in front of him and puts it on her side of the table, sits down.

MAX: Have you ever been to a funeral for a baby?

ETTA: I never have, no.

MAX: The box is so small. You wouldn't believe it. My sister's baby died. It tweaked her. She couldn't stop talking about it. What she'd be doing if she were alive.... You know, learning to crawl, teething...all that.

ETTA: Interesting.

MAX: What about you, you want to have kids?

ETTA: I don't think about it. So maybe I don't.

MAX: You married?

ETTA: I didn't come to talk about myself.

MAX: You're not married. I know all about you, you're not even engaged.

ETTA: Nobody engages me.

MAX (Laughs):   God, I love a woman who can make me laugh. You have no idea how many broads can't crack a joke.

ETTA: It's passive humor. I made a joke off of what you said, it's not like I'm funny, it's more like I'm quick.

MAX: It was a compliment.

ETTA: It was bullshit.

MAX: Have it your way.

ETTA: Twenty is your price.

MAX: Correct.

ETTA: That's high.

MAX: It's mid-range. Plus I have a partner. Safety in numbers, that's why policemen have partners, even if it's a dog. You like dogs?

ETTA: Not really.

MAX: That's too bad 'cause I know a place in Hong Kong serves a very nice dog...ever been to Hong Kong?

ETTA: No.

MAX: You want to go?

ETTA: I hate to fly.

MAX: We could take a boat.

ETTA: Look, I'm sure you're a very nice person but...

MAX: Wait a minute. Are you turning me down?

ETTA: Jesus...look...okay....Forget it... (SHE stands)

MAX: No no no no wait...sit down. (HE takes her hand, pulls her down) Your hands are freezing... (HE rubs her hands in his) You want me to take this job?

ETTA: If you think you can do it.

MAX: If I think....I'm taking it, okay?

ETTA: Fine.

MAX: Your hands aren't getting any warmer.

ETTA: I'll check my pulse...

MAX: You should try a massage...

ETTA: I have to go...

MAX: What do you...wait...what do you want, dating?

ETTA: Look Max, I'm not interested.

MAX (HE lets go): What are you, queer?

ETTA: Yeah, I'm queer, Max, okay?

MAX: No, you're not queer...but I love a woman who lies... they could get their stupid face slapped off lying to me but they don't care. Okay...go. You want to go, go. I happen

to know that I am a very attractive and interesting
person...I can talk to anybody.

ETTA (Beat): You know my business?

MAX: Frankly, it makes me uncomfortable. You're providing a
public service for what I term nuisance individuals, lonely
men who can't stop thinking about their cocks and also I'm a
Catholic and I believe it undermines the stability of the
family, I mean, these men are searching for some lost part
of themselves, i.e. the erotic, the animal, the beast, the
devil, instead of spending the time with their wives and
making sure their children are home instead of ripping off
my fucking radio out of my brand new Porsche and ruining the
console it'll probably cost me two, three thousand dollars
to replace it...

ETTA: I don't date people outside my business because they
expect something that's not there.

MAX: Like what is it?

ETTA: A fantasy.

MAX: About sex?

ETTA: About people.

MAX: Maybe it was never there.

ETTA: It was. That's how I know it's gone.

MAX: Maybe that's why you got in the business.

ETTA: Max, when I look at you...I don't see a human being
anymore. I see meat.

MAX: That's what I see when I look at everybody. I mean, if
you think about it, that's good for me. Not that I had
anything to do with it. I mean...you know, I don't have a
full set of human emotions. Poor parenting during the years
between two and four? I'm not a psycho, like my partner, he
really likes the work, but not me, I'm just sociopathic. I
can still have a good time doing business, but it's an
avocation rather than a calling, you see the difference?

ETTA: I hate sex.

MAX: Me too, it's dirty.

ETTA: I don't want to have sex with you is what I'm saying.

MAX: I don't blame you, I have a disease.

ETTA: Okay, Max. You want to fall in love with me, do it, you probably deserve it.

MAX: Who said anything about love?

ETTA: I'll be in touch.

> SHE moves down right and stands staring out. A moment later ALEC moves down to the table, sits, finishes MAX's drink.

MAX (Chuckles): These bitches, they think they're so tough.

ALEC: Is it on or is it off?

MAX: People crave love, Alec...everywhere you look, hunger, yearning, people are starving for love.

ALEC: Is it on or is it off?

MAX: And yet when it's presented to them, boom, straight-forward, they duck, quack, quack, they wag their head, they say...why me? Suspicious. Why is that?

ALEC: How would I know?

MAX: You ever been in love?

ALEC: Why should I?

MAX: Never mind....Waiter?

> THEY freeze. Blackout.

Scene 17

> Lights flicker across ETTA. BEN enters a moment later. THEY are watching a movie. ETTA moves away, the movie ends. Lights up. BEN is a weird shade of green and is deadly calm.

BEN: It is possible, but not probable. Because it's a particular type of commodity. The price, exorbitant. And you get what you pay for. People, clients, say they can

tell the difference. You can't fake it, that moment the
spirit departs the flesh, you could see for yourself, how
intimate. It makes straight sex look like a kiss on the
cheek.

ETTA: Jesus.

BEN (Sweetly): Don't use that tone of voice, I mean it.

ETTA: I don't like to think you're this kind of human being.

BEN: It's a market Etta. You can't begrudge the market.
You can't wage war on entrepreneurs, can you? You live by
the sword and you die by the same sword Etta. Wise up.
(HE hands her a drink) You look green.

ETTA: I feel sick.

BEN: Wait till you get used to the water.

ETTA: I don't think that's it, water.

BEN: I myself hate philosophy, but if I were you, I'd either
put up or shut up.

ETTA: I don't like myself.

BEN: I have felt that way for years, believe me, you will in
time adjust.

ETTA: You did.

BEN: Yes.

ETTA: And you're happy.

BEN (Thoughtfully): Happiness is not destiny. You must be
happy, no. Even the Founding Fathers wrote, "the pursuit of
of happiness." 'Cause they knew it was a crock. (Smiles)
They were not stupid like most people.

ETTA: If it weren't for you I wouldn't be in this business.

BEN: Oh I don't know. All I did was exploit a situation to
the mutual advantage of us both.

ETTA: You lied.

BEN: Lying is a tricky accusation, Etta. You can say I lied.
I can say you believed the lie. Because deep down inside
you didn't think you could make it. You see what I'm saying,
Etta? It wasn't me that sold you out, it was you.

ETTA: No. It was you.

BEN: Think about it, Etta.

ETTA: No.

BEN (Smiles):   See, it doesn't pay to become circumspect.

ETTA (Beat):   I think you used a friend of mine in a movie.

BEN: We've been using mainly Brazilian prostitutes we buy in
  bulk.

ETTA: James brought her in. She had a tattoo of a snake on
  her back.

BEN: A snake. With its shedding skin...

ETTA: Her name was Sheri...

BEN: I know Sheri.

ETTA: What happened to her?

BEN: We were making a movie. When what is visible becomes
  invisible. Her hair, skin, her eyes go transparent and she
  vanishes. Freaked my fucking film crew out of their gourds.
  I kept waiting for her to come back. But she never did.
  And then I noticed this smell, like gardenias, overpowering
  ...it seemed to hang in the air for hours. (HE takes the
  flower from his lapel)

ETTA: Gardenias, Ben?

BEN: Yes.

ETTA: You like gardenias.

BEN: They're my favorite flower.

          Beat. SHE lights a cigarette.

ETTA: I'll try and remember. The next time I see you I'll be
  sure to bring flowers. (Beat) I have some vendors coming
  in from Seattle I want you to meet.

BEN: What are they vending?

ETTA: Runaways.

BEN: I have all I can use.

ETTA: We can talk.

BEN: I love to talk.

ETTA: They're very well-educated, one of them studied at
Yale. We'll have a nice dinner. You feel like eating, Ben?

BEN: Don't push me, Etta.

ETTA: Good. I'll see you at eight o'clock then.

BEN: Should I dress up or what?

ETTA: I think you should.

BEN: You do.

ETTA: Try and look your best.

BEN (Beat): All right, eight o'clock. I'll see you.

    ETTA crosses, stops, looks at BEN, smiles, then exits.

Scene 18

    MAX stands center, ALEC is staring front, BEN is on
the phone.

MAX: First they had to tear the fence out to get the bulldozer
in to dig the hole, right? The fucking idiots dug the hole
so close to the property line they couldn't drive the dozer
out again, can you believe the intelligence? So these guys
put boards, like plywood, over the hole? Then they try and
drive it out...

ALEC: Max, will you shut up.

MAX: They try and drive it out, right? The bulldozer weighs a
million tons or something on these matchstick boards, of
course it falls in the hole, and they have to get a crane,
coming over my house, it's twenty stories high and arrives
in the middle of the night.

ALEC: Nobody's listening to you.

    BEN hangs up, stares at the phone.

MAX: They take this fucking bulldozer up into the air and then suddenly it drops, straight down on my neighbor's car, a fucking Bentley, right? Antique? He just finished restoring the leather? We're talking about a hundred-thousand-dollar automobile, for Chrissakes! (HE is doubled up laughing)

     The OTHER TWO MEN watch MAX, his laughter subsides.

BEN: I don't know where she could be.

ALEC: Is she always late?

BEN: No.

ALEC: I am starving.

BEN: Can I offer you a drink?

ALEC: I'm not drinking.

MAX: I don't trust a man who doesn't drink, do you, Ben?

BEN: I don't think about it.

MAX: Ben, why don't you have a drink, you need to relax.

BEN: It's 8:30, she should have been here.

MAX: She didn't call...?

BEN: Maybe I should check her room.

ALEC: I don't think so.

MAX: I'll check...oh, wait a minute.

ALEC: I wouldn't.

MAX: Yeah, absolutely. I don't think we should get involved with this...missing person.

BEN: You don't think I should?

ALEC: I wouldn't.

     BEN watches them. MAX and ALEC exchange looks.

MAX: Hey, you know...I'm curious. Why don't you go ahead and check?

BEN: She could be sick, or something, it's better to know than not know. (Crosses to the door) I'll be right back. (Exits)

MAX: Jesus, he's ugly.

ALEC: So where is she?

MAX: She's gone home.

ALEC: Oh.

MAX: She came down to make sure. She's very fair. She's a natural blonde.

ALEC: What, are you thinking of selling her?

MAX: Weren't you?

ALEC: No. She's a very nice woman, a little stiff...but...

MAX: It was a joke. Fair, blonde.

ALEC: God.

MAX: So...you want to wait, eat first...

ALEC: No, we don't wait! Eat, Jesus.

MAX (HE moves around the room, HE stares out downstage): Gee, I'd love to see the museum while I'm here, you know? I've read they have this incredible archeological museum?

ALEC: I'm getting a headache.

MAX: You know the trouble with you? You can't relax, you can't talk, like normal people. Chitchat.

ALEC: Please Max.

MAX: It's civilizing to be able to make small talk, Alec.

BEN (Reenters): She's gone.

MAX: How do you mean?

BEN: Like she was never there. The room is open, the bed is smooth, nothing.

MAX: Amazing. Alec, did you hear what Ben just said?

BEN: It's not like her. She says yes, she says no, it means something.

MAX: So she turned, what are you gonna do, let it ruin your weekend? Shit Ben, grow up.

BEN: I'm disappointed, that's all, to have poured so much of
my time and talent into one individual and to be repaid in
this way...

MAX: I think we know.

BEN: This is weird.

ALEC: What do you say we go get something to eat?

MAX: Yeah, let's go get some grub and do some business.

ALEC: A little food, you'll feel like a new man.

MAX: We thought we'd drive out to La Casita.

BEN: That's a long way to go.

ALEC: I only eat seafood.

BEN: They have a very good turbot right here at the hotel.

ALEC: I only eat shellfish.

BEN: I'm not very hungry.

ALEC: Why don't you just come along to keep us company?

BEN: No.

MAX: I wish you would, Ben, I sincerely do. I think it would
do you a world of good. You don't have to eat, just come out
to be social. Alec is no company at all, and I myself like
to enjoy a good conversation with my meal. What do you say,
Ben? Why don't you come with?

BEN: Why don't you go fuck yourself.

MAX (To ALEC): That's not very nice, is it?

ALEC: No, it's not.

          BEN makes a grab for the phone, ALEC intercepts him.

BEN: I swear to God, if you touch me I'm gonna scream my
fucking head off!

          ALEC rips the receiver cord from the base of the
          phone.

MAX: Touch you, why would we touch you? What are we, queers?
I mean, Alec is queer, but so what...? He never forces

himself on people, at least not ugly slobs like you, you're too old. (ALEC tosses him the cord) You have nothing to fear from Alec.

Blackout.

Scene 19

Lights up on ETTA downstage. SHE is cleaning out her briefcase in a deserted office. SPENCER stands watching her; HE is very tense.

SPENCER: Sheri was a zero, she was a thing.

ETTA: So was Ben.

SPENCER: Ben?! (Snorts) I <u>knew</u> Ben. We went to school... okay? I mean...his mother <u>knew</u> my mother, we used to piss in the same toilet for Chrissake! (Beat) Where are we when women decide it's time to get even. We're talking chaos, extreme situations, danger, danger...danger!

ETTA: You can trust me.

SPENCER: Ben was my friend, Etta.

ETTA: I saw the films he made.

SPENCER: What are you, a critic? Nobody takes those films seriously, they're pictures.

ETTA: They're people.

SPENCER: They're self-hating greedbags who'll do anything for money.

ETTA: Like me.

SPENCER: Did I say you?

ETTA: You meant me...

SPENCER: I meant other women...

ETTA: I am other women.

SPENCER: It's in your heads, if it weren't we'd be out of
 business.

ETTA: I'm out.

SPENCER: Just like that?

ETTA: Exactly.

SPENCER: You killed Ben!

ETTA: What do you want me to say? I'm sorry? I'd like to
 feel sorry. I'd like to feel something. Relief. Revenge.
 I don't feel it. Except for this taste of dirt in my mouth,
 I could be dead. I'm not sorry, Spencer.

        A loud knock. MAX enters.

MAX: I read all the magazines. (HE moves to sit down) Hi,
 Spencer.

SPENCER: Get him out of here.

ETTA: Wait outside.

MAX: What's so top secret?

ETTA: It's business.

MAX (HE nuzzles her): We've got a train to catch.

ETTA: Wait outside.

MAX (Stands, moves off, looks back at SPENCER): You ever been
 to Miami, Spencer? They got a hell of an ocean park down
 there. Dolphins? They're more than a fish. (HE exits)

SPENCER: Don't you ever get sick of hanging out with scum?

ETTA: There's nothing wrong with Max that a lobotomy can't
 cure, but you on the other hand will have to wait for
 evolution.

SPENCER: I suppose if it's funny it's not a problem.

ETTA: It's not funny and I wasn't joking.

SPENCER (Beat): Are you threatening me?

ETTA: I don't know, am I?

SPENCER: Evolution, you think I don't know what that means?

> I know what that means, Etta. Dodo birds. Bald eagles.
> Endangered species...extinction.

ETTA: Fly home, Spencer, your nest is on fire.

SPENCER: I'm not the only one, Etta.

> SPENCER exits. Etta stands, puts on her shoes. A
> loud knock. SHELLY enters with an enormous suitcase.

SHELLY: Are you Emma Jenkins?

ETTA: I might be.

SHELLY: A friend said I could pick up some film work here.

ETTA: A friend.

SHELLY: She thought if I could do one or maybe two movies I
could pay for my headshots and get an agent and put a few
bucks by...

ETTA: We're closed.

SHELLY: She said that you'd be very up-front and not screw me
over. I went to these other agencies run by these Persian
assholes...?

ETTA: Are you deaf or what?

SHELLY: She said she's a good friend of yours. She does
these seminars down in Mexico on out-of-the-body experience.
I saw her do it in front of a bunch of people, she got real
light, like you could see through her and then...poof. It
teaches you how meaningless the body is and how it's never
the thing you remember about people? (Beat) Their bodies?
Hello? Hey.

ETTA: You know, I took this test when I was a kid.

SHELLY: You mean like a screen test?

ETTA: It was a perception test. 'Cause I was quiet my
teacher thought there was something wrong with me. They
show you a bunch of pictures, scenes of daily life, and they
ask you what's happening to see if you know. And I can
remember this one picture, of a woman, floating in the air,
and this magician was pointing at her with his wand. And
they asked me what was happening. And I said the woman is
dead, she's floating to heaven, but my teacher shook her
head and said, no Etta, this is magic, this is a trick. But
what if we were both wrong?

SHELLY: I once read a book about a man who could bend a spoon with his brain.

ETTA: You know what kind of movies get made here?

SHELLY: Look, I think it's kind of a turn-on to be naked in front of men, I mean...they like me and I can make them think I like them, I do it all the time. Not that it's really possible to like them 'cause they're, you know, maggots. But they don't know what I'm thinking, how I laugh at their sick needs. I'm already a great actress, you know what I mean? I bet you trip on this business.

ETTA: How old are you?

SHELLY: Eighteen, but like my stepdad "took me" when I was twelve so you know, I'm not shy. How much do you think I could make anyway?

ETTA: We'd have to see.

SHELLY: Right. (SHE begins to undress) My boyfriend used to cry when I'd take my blouse off. He would just stare at my tits and cry. He was really screwed-up. Don't get shocked 'cause I'm wearing this leather shit underneath...I just came from my other job, I'm a dominant. Listen, do you ever do whip movies? 'Cause I can really use a whip. I just about killed this guy the other night. I start wailin' and forget it's just action. Sometimes I think how it would be to just...well, you know? (Laughs) Sometimes it won't go out of my head. It could be a public service. I bet the city would pay me. (Beat) What do you think?

        ETTA hands SHELLY back her clothes. SHE dresses.

ETTA: I think you'll be able to make upwards of a thousand dollars a day. I think you could do a couple of films with no problem but any more than that and it will hurt your chances of straight film work. I think you have to be very honest with yourself. (SHE pulls a card out of her briefcase, writes on it) You have to see where you fit in the marketplace. Acting is hard work, not for everybody, it's a very tough business. However, in <u>this</u> business, with your looks and your attitude, you could make a small fortune in two or three years, and with good investments, retire.

SHELLY: And do what?

ETTA: Drift. (SHE hands the card to SHELLY)

SHELLY: That doesn't sound like much of a life.

ETTA: Think about it, the business I mean, it's not for everybody.

SHELLY: Right.

> SHELLY picks up her bag, exits. Lights fade out around ETTA, but as SHE speaks the light on her becomes very bright. The sound of an approaching train is heard in the distance. It builds.

ETTA: You have to like to travel. That's the trick to drifting. People you call friends become strangers, one day familiar, the next day better forgotten. You can't want anything, you can't keep anything, because everything... disappears.

> The sound of the train roars by. ETTA vanishes as the lights go to black. The train whistle sounds in the distance.

END OF PLAY

The following is the revised Scene 10 for the Royal
Court production.

Scene 10

    A dance hall. Music. Couples dance. SHERI is
standing downstage fixing her hair. She speaks to ETTA
who is off.

SHERI: Have you ever noticed how some people just can't
  seem to hang onto their money?

      ETTA appears. She stares at her.

ETTA (flatly): No. I never have.

SHERI: It's like they got this hole in their life and
  the money just sort of leaks out.

ETTA: I don't want to talk about this . . .

SHERI: I just thought you made a lot of money.

ETTA: I did.

SHERI: So what happened to all that money?

ETTA: I spent it.

SHERI: On what?

ETTA: I don't remember.

SHERI: Think.

ETTA: Sheri . . .?

SHERI: Clothes?

ETTA: I bought a lot of clothes . . . and a fur coat.

SHERI: In California . . .?

ETTA: I got cold.

SHERI: Shoes?

ETTA: I could never afford to buy good shoes before. . . .

SHERI: You probably had about 30 pairs of shoes. . .

ETTA: I bought a car.

SHERI: Too bad about the car. . .

ETTA: You know those finance companies never even tell
you they're gonna snatch the car, they just come and
take it.

SHERI: You musta sent money home.

ETTA: Oh yeah. . .

SHERI: How much?

ETTA (beat): Not that much.

SHERI: I think if you don't like the way you make money
that you blow it trying to make yourself feel better.

ETTA: Ben screwed me over.

SHERI: You let it happen.

ETTA: Bullshit Sheri.

SHERI: Etta, life has ways of teaching us what we need
to know, intuition is one and disaster is another.
Ladies' choice, Etta.

ETTA: Look at this guy coming in.

     DWIGHT enters.

SHERI: Psycho.

ETTA: His name is Dwight.

SHERI: Dwight, like Norman, strictly from the Bates
Motel.

ETTA: He seems like he's got a lot of money.

SHERI: He's a good looking white guy. He could date
anybody. I mean, except for his eyes, he's handsome.

ETTA: He has a funny arm.

SHERI: Look at his shoes, patent-leather evening pumps,

two hundred and sixty dollars. He's wearing an eight
hundred dollar suit. You have to ask yourself what
this guy is doing paying you twenty-five cents a
minute to dance.

ETTA: He talks.

SHERI: To talk then.

ETTA: He seems like he's lonely.

SHERI: They're always lonely because all their friends
are dead. Oh here comes my dreamboat. He's looking for
me. He's waving . . . (Waves) 'Ola Carlos! (Quiet) You
fat pig . . . (To ETTA) See you later.

     SHERI moves off, DWIGHT steps up to ETTA.

DWIGHT: Hello there, Lana.